CHARLEY
WEAVER'S
FAMILY
ALBUM

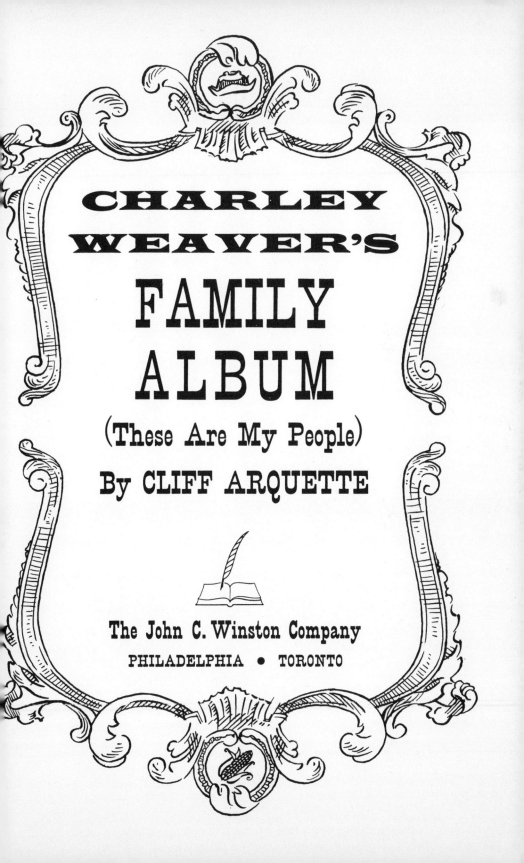

CHARLEY WEAVER'S
FAMILY
ALBUM

(These Are My People)

By CLIFF ARQUETTE

The John C. Winston Company

PHILADELPHIA • TORONTO

Library of Congress Catalog Card Number 60-8818
Made in the United States of America

CHARLEY WEAVER'S FAMILY ALBUM

This is my grandpa, the first Charley Weaver.

Oh, yes, I remember Grandpa. He was in the Civil War where he fought under General Grant, General Lee, General Meade and General Jeb Stuart. He was a pretty mixed-up old man.

This picture was taken the day after he deserted. He didn't mean to desert the army — he thought his commanding officer had given him permission to go. You see he was a bugler and durin' the heat of the battle he ran over to the general and he said, "General, them bullets are gittin' awful thick, what shall I do?" And the general said, "Blow, man, blow." So he did.

He looks like a Weaver, doesn't he? The only reason he grew a beard was because he couldn't find any place on the battle field to plug in his electric razor. Another reason was, nobody had invented electricity yet.

Yes, I remember Grandpa.

This is Grandpa's brother, Gus Weaver. He was the first man in the Civil War to jump out of a balloon at eight hundred feet — without a parachute. Father always said Uncle Gus was the only man he ever knew with accordion-pleated legs. Gus had to give up dancing because his wife's belt buckle scratched his face. His legs were so short he could never catch a streetcar. Father used to say, "With legs that short I doubt if Uncle Gus could catch a cold."

Ten years ago he started to walk over to Lompock — that's three miles from Mount Idy — and as far as we know he hasn't arrived there yet. He's probably playing along the way.

4

This is Grandpa's brother, Colonel Boliver Weaver. He was in the Civil War, too. He was a real fightin' man. Had four swivel chairs shot out from under him.

You can see he's got on a tight collar. He'd eat breakfast, lunch and dinner, and that food wouldn't reach his stomach until night when he'd unbutton his collar. Colonel Weaver didn't talk much durin' the day.

All the Weavers have a strong family resemblance. Take Uncle Boliver here. He's got his mother's eyes, nose, mouth and hair — which left his mother with a pretty blank expression.

After the war he married a big fat woman and they moved into a newly decorated corn-crib three miles south of Mt. Idy.

His wife was so fat she couldn't get life insurance, so she took out group insurance.

During the war he was shot several times; and after the war he was half-shot most of the time.

Yes, indeed, I remember Uncle Boliver.

This is my grandmother, Granny Weaver. She didn't get along too well with Grandpa. She was a good old soul who claimed she'd married a heel.

Her old black dress had more buttons on it than a hi-fi set.

She could outtalk any ten women. Grandpa swears she was vaccinated with a phonograph needle.

She just loved kids. She should. She had a goat farm.

She ruled Grandpa with an iron hand. She sawed it off a statue, and used to belt Grandpa with it. All of us loved Granny — all except Grandpa.

This is my great aunt, Kitty Weaver. She was the first airline stewardess. Aunt Kitty used to say, "In my day, when a stewardess won her wings, she *really* won her wings."

Auntie was hostess for the Hard Cider Flight from Mt. Idy, over Snyder's Swamp to Lompock. From this flight came the aviation term, "flying blind."

In those days the cabins on airplanes were so small the stewardess had to ride outside on the wing. Great Aunt Kitty was promoted for her quick thinking the day the landing gear wouldn't work. She had all the passengers poke their feet through the floor of the plane and run along the runway for a landing.

Her worst day occurred the day some wise guy hung a sign that said Gentlemen on the emergency exit door. They lost seven passengers.

All in all, Auntie loved her work, except for the weekly chore of putting new rubber bands on the engines.

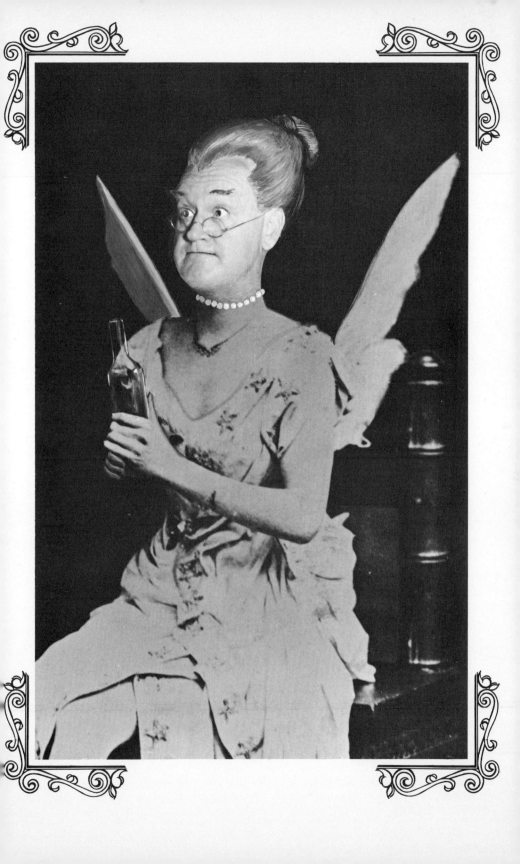

This is a picture of my father when he was a young'un.

I wouldn't say he was fat, but around Christmas time his folks used to hide him for fear somebody might stick an apple in his mouth and roast him.

He was an awfully good baby, but a bit nearsighted. His folks were worried about him because he liked to suck his thumb — they worried even more when he still did it at the age of forty-eight. He claimed it was the only fresh meat he ever got in the house.

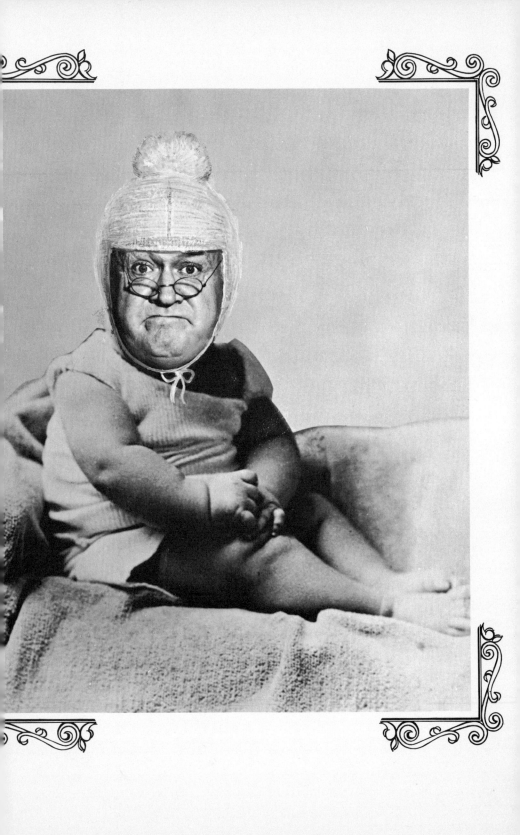

This is Father's sister, Addie Weaver. Auntie never married, although most of her adult life she was asked every day — by her mamma and daddy.

Actually, Addie never cared much for men, but she was nuts about wedding cake.

This picture was made on the two hundred and thirty-third day of her fourteen-day beauty plan.

I remember that Auntie Addie used to threaten to sue her parents for damages every time she looked into a mirror.

14

This is Lyman Fink. He wasn't any relation of mine, but he used to live with us. We treated him just like one of the family — miserably. When he was eleven months old he came into our house looking for his dog. We fed him and he stayed on. The dog left the next day.

Lyman was a gentle fellow but not too bright. He was thirty-seven before he learned to wave "By-by."

Finally, he joined the Army, though he didn't mean to. He just got in a line once, thinking it was a bread line. Instead of bread, they handed him a gun.

He got that first medal on the right for jumping over Niagara Falls. Then he got the big medal for jumping back again. The small one in the middle is a spot of rice pudding.

16

This is a nice picture of Father's half brother, Lem Weaver. Lem was the fastest thing on two wheels in Mt. Idy. He had to be — he was the tax collector.

He once entered a six-day bicycle race, and because he was so fast, he wound it up in three days.

He was never without his bicycle, which complicated things on his wedding night. His wife stood this for six years, then divorced him. She won the custody of the bicycle, but he was allowed to visit it once a week.

He never married again. His spirit was broken.

This is my aunt, Louella Weaver. This picture was taken the night she was crowned Queen of the Woodchopper's Ball. Later, she used to complain of splitting headaches.

That dress she has on is a Paris model. It was sewed by Gertie Paris of Mt. Idy.

Louella was a big girl. She weighed two hundred and eighty pounds. She used to go moose hunting with a hickory switch. She had one of the moose heads mounted and hung on her wall. The first time Father saw it, he said, "That moose sure must have been traveling when he hit the outside of your house, Louella."

Father was never quite well.

This here is Curley Weaver, a distant relative we don't talk about much. He took up the "sports." He had to wear glasses because he was always getting resin in his eyes.

He was fighting a man once, and my father hollered, "Hey Curley, look for an opening." He did. Found one in a fence and went home. The fellow he was fighting was a short little man who only came up to Curley's chin. But he came up there so often! He learned to fight when he was a floorwalker in the Bon Ton basement during Dollar Day.

BROWN BROS.
N.Y.C.

This here is Father's other brother, Elwood, when he and his bride went on their honeymoon to Niagara Falls. Later, his wife said the Falls was her second disappointment.

They were married by a Justice of the Peace, and Elwood always said that was the last time there was any peace in their marriage. They used to fight like cats and dogs — she'd scratch him, and he'd bite her. Even the picture is scratchy.

For twenty years of their married life they never spoke to one another. They had twelve children. Yes, I know what you mean, but then, that branch of the family was always rather unusual.

This is my uncle, Percy Weaver. He was a poet. He never washed his hands. Father said he used to write some pretty dirty poetry, but I thought some of his poems were very good, like: "Mount Idy, Mount Idy, You'll always be tidy," and, "Rickey tic tic, My pig is sick."

He also wrote, "The Wreck of the Hesperus." Later, he claimed somebody stole it and made it famous. He was going to sue the fellow but the judge said there wouldn't be any point in digging up the fellow he wanted to sue; he'd been dead for a hundred years. And Percy said, "O.K. let's attach his salary."

He used to do imitations of birds. He could do a sea gull so real you'd be afraid to look up.

Father used to say he was bull-simple.

26

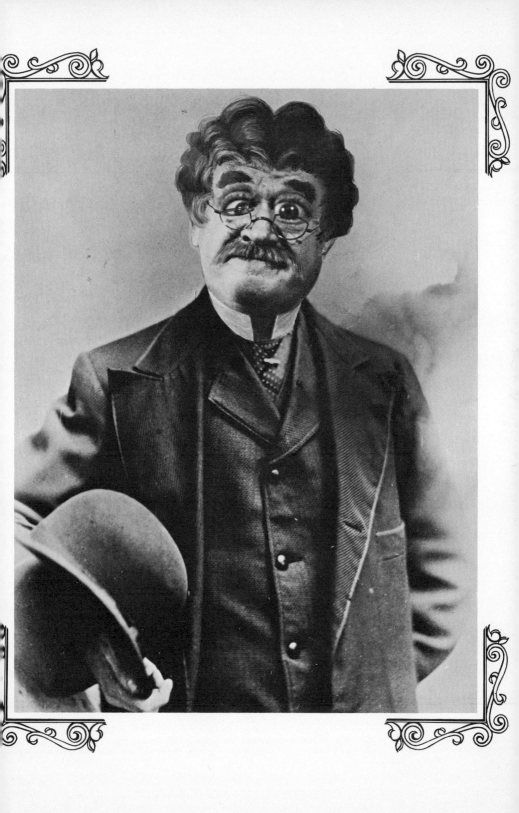

This is Father's cousin, Clem Weaver. He was a soldier in the Civil War and was very brave. He was the first one to run at Bull Run.

He used to carry around a lead "Minnie ball" the doctor dug out of his back. The day he was wounded he created a saying that is still used a great deal. When the doctor started probing for the bullet, he said, "Get the lead out, Doc."

He's now about a hundred and four, and still living — "If you call this living," he says.

28

This here one is a picture of me when I was a baby. For the first year I had snow-white hair. Mamma was so nearsighted she always powdered the wrong end. People used to say I was either the oldest baby or the youngest man they had ever seen. When my father first saw me he went right out and filed a claim for accident insurance.

I was a good baby, but my brother Norby was spoiled. A steam roller ran over him. For several years after that I had a very tall, thin, flat brother.

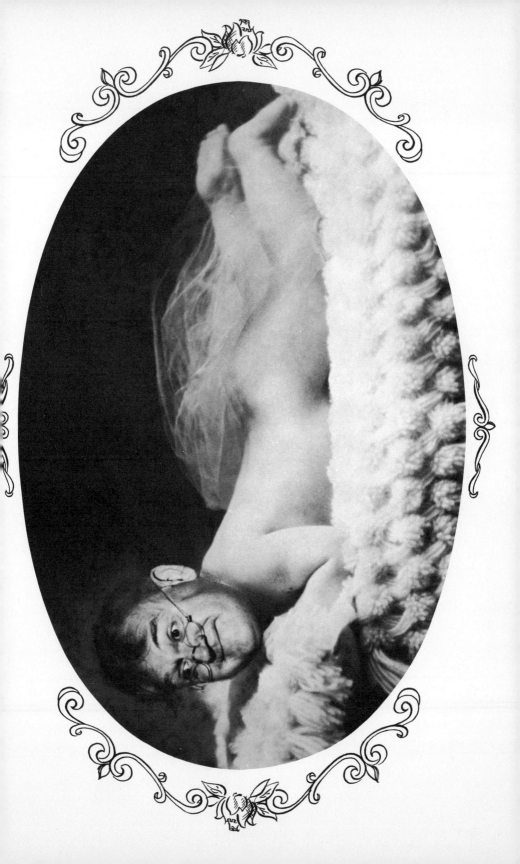

This is me and Mamma and my big brother, Norby. Folks used to say we looked like two peas in a pod — Mamma and me, that is.

Mamma had us all dressed for bed and we were listening to bedtime stories. I can tell you, those stories were real knockouts. Mamma always followed them up by giving us knockout drops.

My, how we used to love to play pat-a-cake! Norby and me used to play pat-a-cake for two or three hours at a time. Mamma didn't like that because we used a real cake.

All in all, though, we were good kids, and all boy.

ere's my little cousin, Willie Sue Weaver. She was very clever with her hands. She knitted that little collar she's wearing. Later, she knitted the chair. In fact, it wasn't safe to get near her if you had a beard. You might wind up with a little sweater on your chin.

Once when the doctor said her father had an iron deficiency she knitted him a pair of socks out of steel wool. She could knit anything.

However, she finally broke her arm and it never did knit. After that, she didn't, either.

This is another cousin of mine, Truman Weaver. He was about eleven when this picture was taken, but he was as simple as a four-year-old. He grew up to be a great politician.

His first job was dogcatcher. In less than two weeks he had caught every dog in Mt. Idy and several strays from Lompock. With no dogs left, he started catching chickens, mostly at night. He was later caught, himself, and soundly thrashed by nine angry farmers.

He later tried to have women in the House of Representatives, so he could call it, the House of Miss-representatives. He lost.

 36

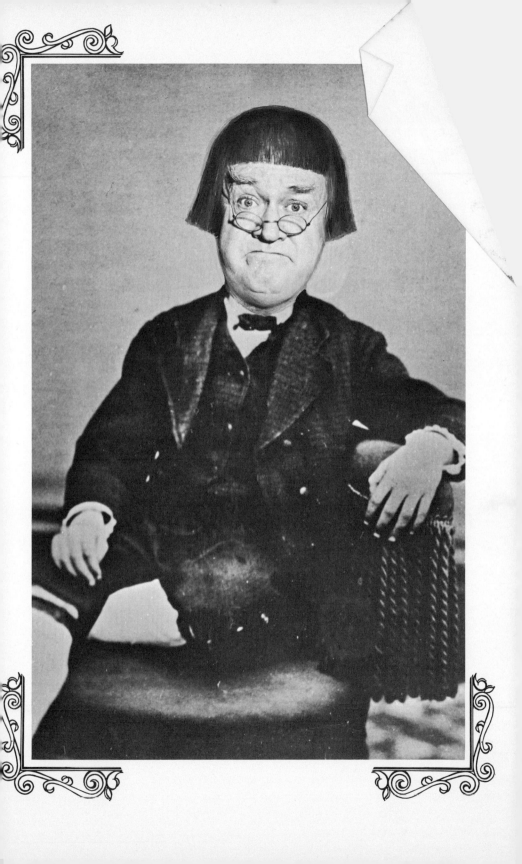

Here are several members of the Weaver family in one picture. Starting on the right side you see my sister, Gladys, who later played fullback for the Rams. Going left, you see my father, Charles Weaver II. He was afraid a snake was going to crawl out of the camera. Leaning on Father's knee is my brother, Norby, fun-loving but mule-simple. Next to Norby is my big sister, George. Mamma had wanted a boy, and Father just couldn't change her mind. Next to George, still reading right to left, is my sister, Fabriolla. She was the first girl in Mt. Idy to slap her boy friend in the face. She only did it once. He chewed tobacco. Then there is Mamma — kind, considerate, patient and alcoholic. Standing back of Mamma is a girl who came to our house looking for her lost kitten. She never found it, but lived with us for twenty-eight years. I don't know what her name was. And the little one on Mamma's lap is me. I was the baby of the family; at that time Mamma had wanted a girl. When you look real close at all of us, ain't it amazing how we all favored Mamma?

This is my little cousin, Thelma Weaver. She was full of spirit, and later when she grew up she was full of spirits — spirits of ammonia, that is. She was pretty far gone when this picture was taken. The truth is, she had just fallen out of the third story window. That's how she acquired her taste for spirits. Her mother gave her some to revive her.

When this picture was taken you could give her a whiff and she'd dance and sing and carry on like a grown woman. She's still living, and now she dances and sings and carries on like a little girl.

This is a picture of me on my ninth birthday. Grandpa had just given me this little bow and arrow. So — I shot him.

Here's my brother, Norby. He had a good head on his shoulders. We never could figure out who's head it was, though. This picture was taken the day he graduated into the third grade. Norby could lick any kid his size in his class. He didn't have many fights, though, because all the kids his size were in high school.

Norby is sitting on the famous Mt. Idy kissing rock. They say if you sit there long enough a beautiful girl will come by and kiss you. We all went out there the other day to see him on the rock and help him celebrate his eighty-fourth birthday.

This is my oldest sister, Gladys Willie. She's tryin' to pretend she's "September Morn" (that famous painting).

Father never liked this picture. Said she looked as naked as a jaybird. This was taken during high tide at Snyder's Swamp.

Another reason Father didn't like this picture was because she was standing on his head when it was taken. We squoze water out of him for three days after it was over.

Gladys wanted to be a skin diver but Father wouldn't let her. He says who would she sell skin to after she found it?

We all worry about Father.

46

This is my brother, Russell Weaver. He was the best baker in Mount Idy. Mamma used to say he ought to be the best — he certainly knew how to loaf. Right now he's got a big piece of cake in his mouth. He said he wanted to have a sweet expression on his face when he had his picture took.

Mamma never cared much for his pies. He made one for her once and it had a big lump in the middle of it. When he explained to Mamma that a mouse got in the pie, she said a mouse wouldn't make that big a lump. And he said he put a cat in to catch the mouse.

He made awful good pretzels, but he had to quit making them because he got the bends.

But you know, when I look through my old family album, the one I remember most is my sister, Winnie Ethel Weaver. Fun-loving, carefree and vicious to a fault. She was in the show business.

She left home when she was nine years old after a slight disagreement with my father. Fractured both his arms. Next thing we heard of her she was appearing on the stage in New York in an act called "Winsome Winnie Weaver — World's Weirdest Weight Lifter."

Yes, she was strong all right, in more ways than one. In one part of her act she used to stand on a cement block while her assistant (fellow named Slug) would hit her on top of the head with a forty-pound sledge hammer and break the cement block. She finally had to cut that part out of her act because she started to get fallen arches.

Yes, I remember Mamma, Father and my brothers and sisters, but most of all — I remember Winnie!

This is a picture of me, Charley Weaver, taken on my eighteenth birthday. The photographer fella said, "Watch the birdie." Instead of my seeing it, he gave it to me.

That suit was the nicest one I ever had. It came complete with a bat and a catcher's mitt. I wore that suit for — I wore that suit for — what *did* I wear that suit for?

I didn't really smoke that pipe, but it made a nice thing to carry my Sen Sen in.

52

ere's another picture of me, Charley Weaver III, taken the day I was fourteen and went into uniform. I was head usher at the Bijou Theater and I ran the buttered kumquat concession. I even remember the picture that was playing that week, it was called, *I Was A Teen-age Ox*. Starring Mary Miles Gummerson, it was the story of a three-year-old girl's fight against the United States government. The companion picture was a Western entitled, *I Was A Teen-age Mule*. But it starred Rex, the wild horse. Rex was only in one short scene; I guess that's why he was so wild.

As you can see by my picture, I had long curly black hair. Not because I wanted it — that spring a blue-bellied woodpecker built her nest in my hair. You see, I couldn't chase her out for two reasons — one, I'm a bird lover; and two, she would have pecked my brains out. I didn't mind it so much until she started giving parties and inviting friends. Yes, I rem —

Oh that's me.

54

This picture of my sister, Bessie, was taken the day she and her husband separated.

This is a picture of me the day I married my little wife, Beryl. That ain't Beryl in the picture, though. It was a friend of Beryl's. You see, Beryl took such a bad picture she had her friend stand in for her.